AUTO RECORD BOOK

Copyright 2014

GAS AND OIL CONSUMPTION

DATE	MILEAGE READING	GALS.	COST	MILES per GAL,

GAS AND OIL CONSUMPTION

DATE	MILEAGE READING	GALS.	COST	MILES per GAL,

GAS AND OIL CONSUMPTION

DATE	MILEAGE READING	GALS.	COST	MILES per GAL,

GAS AND OIL CONSUMPTION

DATE	MILEAGE READING	GALS.	COST	MILES per GAL,

GAS AND OIL CONSUMPTION

DATE	MILEAGE READING	GALS.	COST	MILES per GAL,

GAS AND OIL CONSUMPTION

DATE	MILEAGE READING	GALS.	COST	MILES per GAL,

GAS AND OIL CONSUMPTION

DATE	MILEAGE READING	GALS.	COST	MILES per GAL,

GAS AND OIL CONSUMPTION

DATE	MILEAGE READING	GALS.	COST	MILES per GAL,

GAS AND OIL CONSUMPTION

DATE	MILEAGE READING	GALS.	COST	MILES per GAL,

GAS AND OIL CONSUMPTION

DATE	MILEAGE READING	GALS.	COST	MILES per GAL,

GAS AND OIL CONSUMPTION

DATE	MILEAGE READING	GALS.	COST	MILES per GAL,

GAS AND OIL CONSUMPTION

DATE	MILEAGE READING	GALS.	COST	MILES per GAL,

GAS AND OIL CONSUMPTION

DATE	MILEAGE READING	GALS.	COST	MILES per GAL,

GAS AND OIL CONSUMPTION

DATE	MILEAGE READING	GALS.	COST	MILES per GAL,

GAS AND OIL CONSUMPTION

DATE	MILEAGE READING	GALS.	COST	MILES per GAL,

GAS AND OIL CONSUMPTION

DATE	MILEAGE READING	GALS.	COST	MILES per GAL,

GAS AND OIL CONSUMPTION

DATE	MILEAGE READING	GALS.	COST	MILES per GAL,

GAS AND OIL CONSUMPTION

DATE	MILEAGE READING	GALS.	COST	MILES per GAL,

GAS AND OIL CONSUMPTION

DATE	MILEAGE READING	GALS.	COST	MILES per GAL,

GAS AND OIL CONSUMPTION

DATE	MILEAGE READING	GALS.	COST	MILES per GAL,

GAS AND OIL CONSUMPTION

DATE	MILEAGE READING	GALS.	COST	MILES per GAL,

GAS AND OIL CONSUMPTION

DATE	MILEAGE READING	GALS.	COST	MILES per GAL,

GAS AND OIL CONSUMPTION

DATE	MILEAGE READING	GALS.	COST	MILES per GAL,

GAS AND OIL CONSUMPTION

DATE	MILEAGE READING	GALS.	COST	MILES per GAL,

GAS AND OIL CONSUMPTION

DATE	MILEAGE READING	GALS.	COST	MILES per GAL,

GAS AND OIL CONSUMPTION

DATE	MILEAGE READING	GALS.	COST	MILES per GAL,

GAS AND OIL CONSUMPTION

DATE	MILEAGE READING	GALS.	COST	MILES per GAL,

GAS AND OIL CONSUMPTION

DATE	MILEAGE READING	GALS.	COST	MILES per GAL,

GAS AND OIL CONSUMPTION

DATE	MILEAGE READING	GALS.	COST	MILES per GAL,

GAS AND OIL CONSUMPTION

DATE	MILEAGE READING	GALS.	COST	MILES per GAL,

GAS AND OIL CONSUMPTION

DATE	MILEAGE READING	GALS.	COST	MILES per GAL,

GAS AND OIL CONSUMPTION

DATE	MILEAGE READING	GALS.	COST	MILES per GAL,

GAS AND OIL CONSUMPTION

DATE	MILEAGE READING	GALS.	COST	MILES per GAL,

GAS AND OIL CONSUMPTION

DATE	MILEAGE READING	GALS.	COST	MILES per GAL,

GAS AND OIL CONSUMPTION

DATE	MILEAGE READING	GALS.	COST	MILES per GAL,

GAS AND OIL CONSUMPTION

DATE	MILEAGE READING	GALS.	COST	MILES per GAL,

GAS AND OIL CONSUMPTION

DATE	MILEAGE READING	GALS.	COST	MILES per GAL,

GAS AND OIL CONSUMPTION

DATE	MILEAGE READING	GALS.	COST	MILES per GAL,

GAS AND OIL CONSUMPTION

DATE	MILEAGE READING	GALS.	COST	MILES per GAL,

GAS AND OIL CONSUMPTION

DATE	MILEAGE READING	GALS.	COST	MILES per GAL,

GAS AND OIL CONSUMPTION

DATE	MILEAGE READING	GALS.	COST	MILES per GAL,

GAS AND OIL CONSUMPTION

DATE	MILEAGE READING	GALS.	COST	MILES per GAL,

GAS AND OIL CONSUMPTION

DATE	MILEAGE READING	GALS.	COST	MILES per GAL,

GAS AND OIL CONSUMPTION

DATE	MILEAGE READING	GALS.	COST	MILES per GAL,

GAS AND OIL CONSUMPTION

DATE	MILEAGE READING	GALS.	COST	MILES per GAL.

GAS AND OIL CONSUMPTION

DATE	MILEAGE READING	GALS.	COST	MILES per GAL,

GAS AND OIL CONSUMPTION

DATE	MILEAGE READING	GALS.	COST	MILES per GAL,

GAS AND OIL CONSUMPTION

DATE	MILEAGE READING	GALS.	COST	MILES per GAL,

GAS AND OIL CONSUMPTION

DATE	MILEAGE READING	GALS.	COST	MILES per GAL,

GAS AND OIL CONSUMPTION

DATE	MILEAGE READING	GALS.	COST	MILES per GAL,

GAS AND OIL CONSUMPTION

DATE	MILEAGE READING	GALS.	COST	MILES per GAL,

GAS AND OIL CONSUMPTION

DATE	MILEAGE READING	GALS.	COST	MILES per GAL,

GAS AND OIL CONSUMPTION

DATE	MILEAGE READING	GALS.	COST	MILES per GAL,

GAS AND OIL CONSUMPTION

DATE	MILEAGE READING	GALS.	COST	MILES per GAL,

GAS AND OIL CONSUMPTION

DATE	MILEAGE READING	GALS.	COST	MILES per GAL,

GAS AND OIL CONSUMPTION

DATE	MILEAGE READING	GALS.	COST	MILES per GAL,

GAS AND OIL CONSUMPTION

DATE	MILEAGE READING	GALS.	COST	MILES per GAL,

GAS AND OIL CONSUMPTION

DATE	MILEAGE READING	GALS.	COST	MILES per GAL,

GAS AND OIL CONSUMPTION

DATE	MILEAGE READING	GALS.	COST	MILES per GAL,

GAS AND OIL CONSUMPTION

DATE	MILEAGE READING	GALS.	COST	MILES per GAL,

GAS AND OIL CONSUMPTION

DATE	MILEAGE READING	GALS.	COST	MILES per GAL,

GAS AND OIL CONSUMPTION

DATE	MILEAGE READING	GALS.	COST	MILES per GAL,

GAS AND OIL CONSUMPTION

DATE	MILEAGE READING	GALS.	COST	MILES per GAL,

GAS AND OIL CONSUMPTION

DATE	MILEAGE READING	GALS.	COST	MILES per GAL,

GAS AND OIL CONSUMPTION

DATE	MILEAGE READING	GALS.	COST	MILES per GAL,

GAS AND OIL CONSUMPTION

DATE	MILEAGE READING	GALS.	COST	MILES per GAL,

GAS AND OIL CONSUMPTION

DATE	MILEAGE READING	GALS.	COST	MILES per GAL,

GAS AND OIL CONSUMPTION

DATE	MILEAGE READING	GALS.	COST	MILES per GAL,

GAS AND OIL CONSUMPTION

DATE	MILEAGE READING	GALS.	COST	MILES per GAL,

GAS AND OIL CONSUMPTION

DATE	MILEAGE READING	GALS.	COST	MILES per GAL,

GAS AND OIL CONSUMPTION

DATE	MILEAGE READING	GALS.	COST	MILES per GAL.

GAS AND OIL CONSUMPTION

DATE	MILEAGE READING	GALS.	COST	MILES per GAL,

GAS AND OIL CONSUMPTION

DATE	MILEAGE READING	GALS.	COST	MILES per GAL,

GAS AND OIL CONSUMPTION

DATE	MILEAGE READING	GALS.	COST	MILES per GAL,

GAS AND OIL CONSUMPTION

DATE	MILEAGE READING	GALS.	COST	MILES per GAL,

GAS AND OIL CONSUMPTION

DATE	MILEAGE READING	GALS.	COST	MILES per GAL,

GAS AND OIL CONSUMPTION

DATE	MILEAGE READING	GALS.	COST	MILES per GAL,

GAS AND OIL CONSUMPTION

DATE	MILEAGE READING	GALS.	COST	MILES per GAL,

GAS AND OIL CONSUMPTION

DATE	MILEAGE READING	GALS.	COST	MILES per GAL,

GAS AND OIL CONSUMPTION

DATE	MILEAGE READING	GALS.	COST	MILES per GAL,

GAS AND OIL CONSUMPTION

DATE	MILEAGE READING	GALS.	COST	MILES per GAL,

GAS AND OIL CONSUMPTION

DATE	MILEAGE READING	GALS.	COST	MILES per GAL,

GAS AND OIL CONSUMPTION

DATE	MILEAGE READING	GALS.	COST	MILES per GAL,

GAS AND OIL CONSUMPTION

DATE	MILEAGE READING	GALS.	COST	MILES per GAL,

GAS AND OIL CONSUMPTION

DATE	MILEAGE READING	GALS.	COST	MILES per GAL,

GAS AND OIL CONSUMPTION

DATE	MILEAGE READING	GALS.	COST	MILES per GAL,

GAS AND OIL CONSUMPTION

DATE	MILEAGE READING	GALS.	COST	MILES per GAL,

GAS AND OIL CONSUMPTION

DATE	MILEAGE READING	GALS.	COST	MILES per GAL,

GAS AND OIL CONSUMPTION

DATE	MILEAGE READING	GALS.	COST	MILES per GAL,

GAS AND OIL CONSUMPTION

DATE	MILEAGE READING	GALS.	COST	MILES per GAL,

GAS AND OIL CONSUMPTION

DATE	MILEAGE READING	GALS.	COST	MILES per GAL,

GAS AND OIL CONSUMPTION

DATE	MILEAGE READING	GALS.	COST	MILES per GAL,

GAS AND OIL CONSUMPTION

DATE	MILEAGE READING	GALS.	COST	MILES per GAL,

GAS AND OIL CONSUMPTION

DATE	MILEAGE READING	GALS.	COST	MILES per GAL,

GAS AND OIL CONSUMPTION

DATE	MILEAGE READING	GALS.	COST	MILES per GAL,

GAS AND OIL CONSUMPTION

DATE	MILEAGE READING	GALS.	COST	MILES per GAL,

GAS AND OIL CONSUMPTION

DATE	MILEAGE READING	GALS.	COST	MILES per GAL,

GAS AND OIL CONSUMPTION

DATE	MILEAGE READING	GALS.	COST	MILES per GAL,